INDIANA

The Hoosier State

BY
JOHN HAMILTON

Abdo & Daughters
An imprint of Abdo Publishing | abdopublishing.com

abdopublishing.com

Published by ABDO Publishing, a division of ABDO, PO Box 398166, Minneapolis, Minnesota 55439. Copyright © 2017 by Abdo Consulting Group, Inc. International copyrights reserved in all countries. No part of this book may be reproduced in any form without written permission from the publisher. ABDO & Daughters™ is a trademark and logo of ABDO Publishing.

Printed in the United States of America, North Mankato, Minnesota.
012016
092016

THIS BOOK CONTAINS
RECYCLED MATERIALS

Editor: Sue Hamilton   **Contributing Editor:** Bridget O'Brien
Graphic Design: Sue Hamilton
Cover Art Direction: Candice Keimig   **Cover Photo Selection:** Neil Klinepier
Cover Photo: iStock
Interior Images: Alamy, AP, ArcelorMittal, Children's Museum of Indianapolis, Corbis, Dreamstime, Granger, Herb Row, History in Full Color-Restoration/Colorization, Indiana Pacers, Indianapolis Colts, Indy Jazz Fest, iStock, Library of Congress, Lynne Whitehorn-Umphres, Mark Lemmon, Mile High Maps, Mountain High Maps, North Wind Picture Archives, One Mile Up, Peter Arnold, Santa Claus Indiana Post Office, Science Source, U.S. Postal Service.

Statistics: *State and City Populations*, U.S. Census Bureau, July 1, 2014 estimates; *Land and Water Area*, U.S. Census Bureau, 2010 Census, MAF/TIGER database; *State Temperature Extremes*, NOAA National Climatic Data Center; *Climatology and Average Annual Precipitation*, NOAA National Climatic Data Center, 1980-2015 statewide averages; *State Highest and Lowest Points*, NOAA National Geodetic Survey.

Websites: To learn more about the United States, visit booklinks.abdopublishing.com. These links are routinely monitored and updated to provide the most current information available.

Cataloging-in-Publication Data

Names: Hamilton, John, 1959- author.
Title: Indiana / by John Hamilton.
Description: Minneapolis, MN : Abdo Publishing, [2017] | Series: The United
    States of America | Includes index.
Identifiers: LCCN 2015957603 | ISBN 9781680783162 (lib. bdg.) |
    ISBN 9781680774207 (ebook)
Subjects: LCSH: Indiana--Juvenile literature.
Classification: DDC 977.2--dc23
LC record available at http://lccn.loc.gov/2015957603

CONTENTS

THE HOOSIER STATE

Driving through the flat plains of central Indiana, one might think the state is nothing more than endless fields of corn and soybeans. But Indiana is a land of variety. In the south are hilly forests. In the north, sand dunes along the shores of Lake Michigan share the spotlight with industrialized cities. Farming is important to Indiana, but the leading industry is manufacturing. Indiana is the number-one steel producing state in the nation.

Indiana is called "The Hoosier State," and nobody really knows why. It might be an 1800s term for a backwoodsman, but there are many explanations. Whatever the original meaning, the state's residents like calling themselves Hoosiers.

One thing everybody agrees on is that Hoosiers love sports. From the Indianapolis 500 auto race to high school basketball, Indiana is famous for the loyalty of its sports fans.

The Indianapolis 500 auto race is held every year in May. The race is called "The Greatest Spectacle in Racing."

QUICK FACTS

Name: Indiana is an English word that means "Land of the Indians."

State Capital: Indianapolis, population 848,788

Date of Statehood: December 11, 1816 (19th state)

Population: 6,596,855 (16th-most populous state)

Area (Total Land and Water): 36,420 square miles (94,327 sq km), 38th-largest state

Largest City: Indianapolis, population 848,788

Nickname: The Hoosier State

Motto: The Crossroads of America

State Bird: Cardinal

State Flower: Peony

State Rock: Salem Limestone

State Tree: Tulip Tree

State Song: "On the Banks of the Wabash, Far Away"

Highest Point: Hoosier Hill, 1,257 feet (383 m)

Lowest Point: 320 feet (98 m) on the Ohio River

Average July High Temperature: 85°F (29°C)

Record High Temperature: 116°F (47°C), in Collegeville on July 14, 1936

Average January Low Temperature: 19°F (-7°C)

Record Low Temperature: -36°F (-38°C), in New Whiteland on January 19, 1994

Average Annual Precipitation: 42 inches (107 cm)

Number of U.S. Senators: 2

Number of U.S. Representatives: 9

U.S. Postal Service Abbreviation: IN

GEOGRAPHY

Indiana is the 38th-largest state. It is in the upper Midwest region of the United States. The state is divided into two geographical parts. These include the northern two-thirds and the southern third of the state. The northern region is mostly flat. In the south, there are some rugged hills.

During the last Ice Age, starting about 50,000 years ago, glaciers covered most of today's northern and central Indiana. When they finally melted, they left behind a mostly flat landscape. After centuries of grasslands growing and dying, the soil became enriched. Indiana has some of the most fertile soil in the country.

Today, the northern two-thirds of Indiana is mostly flat, fertile farmland.

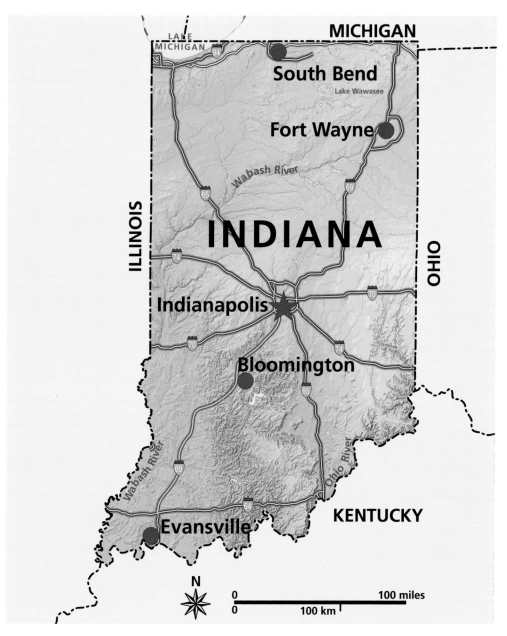

MICHIGAN

LAKE MICHIGAN

South Bend

Lake Wawasee

Fort Wayne

Wabash River

65

69

ILLINOIS

INDIANA

OHIO

74

Indianapolis

70

70

74

Bloomington

65

Wabash River

69

Ohio River

64

KENTUCKY

Evansville

N

0   100 miles
0   100 km

Indiana's total land and water area is 36,420 square miles (94,327 sq km). It is the 38th-largest state. The state capital is Indianapolis.

Indiana is shaped roughly like a rectangle. It is about 250 miles (402 km) from north to south, but just 145 miles (233 km) from east to west. Bordering Indiana to the north is the state of Michigan. To the west is Illinois. Indiana shares its southern border with Kentucky. To the east is Ohio.

South-central Indiana was mostly untouched by the glacial scouring of the last Ice Age. As a result, this region has rugged, forested hills and deep valleys. There are also many limestone caves.

Clifty Creek flows across a limestone bed and through a steep-walled valley, creating Anderson Falls in south-central Indiana.

Much of Indiana's Lake Michigan shoreline is used by various industries. However, the Indiana Dunes National Lakeshore is a 15-mile (24-km) protected area used for recreation.

Lake Michigan is on Indiana's northwest corner. Access to the Great Lakes helps Indiana's industrial development and transportation network. There are massive sand dunes along parts of the shore. A 15-mile (24-km) stretch of shoreline has been saved from development by the creation in 1966 of the Indiana Dunes National Lakeshore.

Indiana's official state river is the winding Wabash River. It flows through the state's north-central region. It then forms the state's southwestern border with Illinois before draining into the Ohio River.

The Ohio River is another major Indiana waterway. It forms the state's southern border with Kentucky. It is used extensively to ship bulky cargo in large barges. Other important Indiana waterways include the Kankakee, Maumee, Tippecanoe, White, Mississinewa, St. Joseph, and Whitewater Rivers.

There are about 900 lakes in Indiana. The largest natural lake within the state's borders is Lake Wawasee.

GEOGRAPHY

CLIMATE AND
WEATHER

Indiana is in the north-central part of the United States. Because of this, it has a humid continental climate. The state usually has hot summers and cold, snowy winters. In the very southern part of Indiana, temperatures are usually milder, with less snow.

A father and son face blowing winds and snow to go sledding on a golf course in Evansville, Indiana.

Indiana's average yearly rainfall measures 42 inches (107 cm). In the summer months, thunderstorms often rumble overhead. Severe weather such as hailstorms and tornados sometimes strike the state. Tornados are more frequent in the spring. In winter, blizzards can be a hazard.

Indiana's average July high temperature is 85°F (29°C). The mercury once climbed to a record 116°F (47°C) in Collegeville on July 14, 1936. In January, the average low temperature is 19°F (-7°C). On January 19, 1994, the thermometer sank to a record low of -36°F (-38°C) in New Whiteland.

CLIMATE AND WEATHER

PLANTS AND ANIMALS

There are more than 85 different kinds of trees growing in Indiana's rich soil. The most common trees include oak, hickory, ash, maple, walnut, and cherry. Most are deciduous trees, with broad leaves that turn color in the fall and then drop before winter. There are very few softwood or evergreen trees in the state.

Deciduous trees line the banks of Mill Creek in Owen County, Indiana.

14

Tulip Tree Blossom

Peony

Virginia Bluebells

The tulip tree (also called the tulip poplar) is Indiana's official state tree. Its yellow blossoms look like tulips. The trees grow quickly and have sturdy wood. Earlier in Indiana's history, Native Americans used the wood to make canoes. Today, it is used to make cabinets and furniture.

In the spring, Indiana wildflowers bloom and carpet the state's prairies and woodlands. They include common blue violet, prairie trillium, spiderwort, Virginia bluebells, and wild ginger. The official state flower is the peony. These pink, red, white, or yellow flowers bloom in late spring.

PLANTS AND ANIMALS

Indiana bats spend the winter months hibernating in caves and mines. The small bats are endangered animals, but have been making a comeback.

There are many kinds of animals found in Indiana. Most are common to the states of the Midwest and eastern United States. They include white-tailed deer, chipmunks, opossums, minks, raccoons, muskrats, bats, badgers, rabbits, squirrels, mice, beavers, bobcats, coyotes, foxes, moles, river otters, and shrews.

Birds are often seen perched on tree branches or fence posts in Indiana. The official state bird is the cardinal. Males are colored brilliant scarlet red. They are territorial birds, and can be seen year-round. Other common birds roosting in Indiana include swallows, starlings, ruby-throated hummingbirds, mourning doves, chickadees, sandhill cranes, bluebirds, robins, sparrows, and orioles. Gulls are found along the shores of Lake Michigan.

Eastern box turtles were once popular pets, but are now protected in Indiana. They may live 30 to 40 years in the wild and 80 to 100 years in captivity.

Even though much of Indiana's crucial wetlands have decreased in the past century, there are still many kinds of reptiles and amphibians found in the state. Common snakes include bull snakes, garter snakes, and black kingsnakes. Venomous snakes are rare, but northern copperheads, western cottonmouths, and timber rattlesnakes are sometimes found in the state. Other common reptiles of Indiana include broadhead skinks, Eastern fence lizards, and Eastern box turtles. The state's wetlands are also home to many kinds of amphibians such as frogs, toads, mudpuppies, newts, and salamanders.

Many kinds of fish swim in Indiana's lakes and rivers. They include sunfish, smallmouth and largemouth bass, trout, muskie, walleye, catfish, gar, darter, northern pike, bluegill, steelhead, crappie, and yellow perch.

HISTORY

Indiana is a word that means "Land of the Indians." The ancestors of today's Native Americans first settled the area about 10,000 years ago, after the glaciers from the last Ice Age melted. They used stone tools for hunting and woodworking. Starting around 1000 AD, people of the Mississippian Culture gathered in settlements. They grew corn and squash.

Angel Mounds is a preserved Mississippian Culture settlement near Evansville, Indiana. Built between 1050 and 1400 AD, it became home to nearly 1,000 Native Americans. The site was abandoned before Europeans arrived.

They also built large earthen mounds for religious purposes.

By the time French explorers arrived in the late 1600s, the land was settled mainly by three groups of Native Americans. They included the Miami, Illini, and Shawnee tribes.

French fur traders built forts in the early 1700s. They were located near the present-day cities of Fort Wayne, Lafayette, and Vincennes. The French traded blankets, tools, weapons, and other goods to Native Americans in exchange for valuable fur pelts. British traders soon entered the area. They also wanted to trade for furs. Fighting often broke out between the French and British.

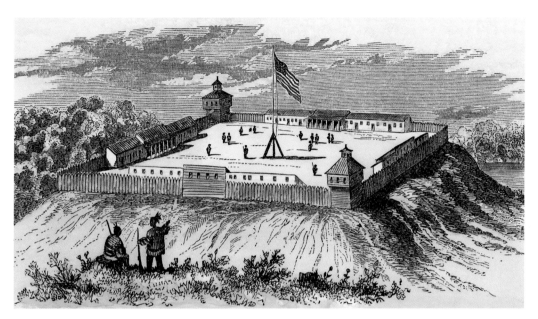

Above: An illustration of the original Fort Wayne, built in the early 1800s. The all-wooden fort was designed to be defended against attack by only 50-75 troops.

Below: Today a recreation of Fort Wayne stands close to its original location near the city of Fort Wayne, Indiana. Visitors can come to the "Old Fort." It is manned by actors who dress and work as though they are members of a 19th-century military trading post.

In the mid-1700s, France and Great Britain fought battles over their North American territories. The French and Indian War lasted from 1754 to 1763. Great Britain won the war. France lost its lands east of the Mississippi River, including Indiana.

In 1775, Great Britain went to war against its American colonies, which wanted independence. In 1783, Great Britain lost the American Revolution. Indiana changed hands again. It became part of the newly formed United States.

In the late 1780s, Indiana was part of the Northwest Territory. It included the present-day states of Indiana, Ohio, Illinois, Michigan, Wisconsin, and a part of Minnesota.

In the 1780s, Indiana was part of the Northwest Territory. Indiana become a state on December 11, 1816.

In 1811, General William Harrison gathered about 1,000 U.S. Army and militia troops near the Tippecanoe River, in Indiana Territory. They were attacked on November 7 by a Shawnee-led group of Native Americans. Both sides suffered losses, but the Native Americans were forced to flee. This became known as the Battle of Tippecanoe.

Indiana's Native Americans fought to keep their lands from being taken by American settlers. A group called the Miami Confederacy won some early battles, but in 1794 they were crushed at the Battle of Fallen Timbers, near the present-day Ohio-Indiana border. General "Mad" Anthony Wayne led the United States troops.

The Northwest Territory was split into smaller parts in 1800. One was called Indiana Territory. Native Americans continued fighting against new settlers. In 1811, future President William Henry Harrison led U.S. troops and defeated a group of Native American tribes at the Battle of Tippecanoe. Most Indiana Native Americans were forced to move to lands west of the Mississippi River.

On December 11, 1816, Indiana became a state. It was the 19th state to enter the Union.

By the mid-1800s, Indiana had become an important center of trade. The state's farms produced massive amounts of corn, wheat, and livestock such as cattle and hogs. These products were easily transported along the Ohio River and on Lake Michigan, eventually reaching cities all across the country.

During the Civil War (1861-1865), Indiana troops fought on the side of the Union. Indiana opposed slavery. More than 200,000 Indianans fought in the war.

In the late 1800s and early 1900s, a prosperous Indiana began to industrialize, especially in the northern part of the state. More roads and railroads were built, and canals dug, making it easier than ever for the state's factories to ship products. Many carmakers built factories in Indiana. The state's first steel mill began construction in 1906 in Gary, Indiana.

Elwood Haynes of Kokomo, Indiana, with the help of machine shop owners Elmer and Edgar Apperson, built the Haynes "Pioneer" automobile in 1894.

During World War I (1914-1918) and World War II (1939-1945), Indiana helped supply the country and its allies with food and factory goods.

After World War II, the state's population continued to grow. However, the economy shrank during the 1970s, forcing many car factories and other companies to go out of business.

Starting in the 1980s, Indiana diversified its economy. It no longer depended solely on heavy industry or agriculture. Financial services, health care, and the making of medicines also became important. Today, the state's economy continues to grow.

A welder works at an Indiana steel mill in 1942, during World War II.

DID YOU KNOW?

- Goldfish bought in pet stores are not wild. They are raised on fish farms. The first successful fish farm was Grassyfork Fisheries in Martinsville, Indiana. It opened in 1899 with just 200 fish. Owner Eugene Curtis Shireman grew the business until it became the world's largest goldfish hatchery. Today, the building is on the National Register of Historic Places.

- A captured German "buzz bomb" from World War II is displayed in front of the Greencastle, Indiana, courthouse. It is one of only two buzz bombs in the United States (the other is at the Smithsonian Institution in Washington, DC). Officially called the V-1, thousands of these pilotless guided bombs were launched against London and other targets in Great Britain from 1944-1945. They were called buzz bombs because of the terrible screeching noise they made.

- Greensburg, Indiana, is nicknamed "Tree City." There are two mulberry trees growing from the 115-foot (35-m) clock tower on top of the Decatur County Courthouse. Trees somehow

took root on the roof in 1870. They have been pruned over the years, and some have died. Two continue growing on the roof today.

• Each Christmas, thousands of letters addressed to Santa Claus wind up in the tiny post office of Santa Claus, Indiana. Letters arrive from all over the world. "Santa's elves" make sure each child gets a reply from Santa Claus. More than 13,000 letters are answered each year. This small southern Indiana town was first settled in the 1850s. Its original name was Santa Fe, Indiana. In 1856, residents applied for a town post office. The United States Postal Service refused because there was already a Santa Fe in New Mexico. After talking it over, the Indiana residents decided to change their town's name to Santa Claus. Holiday World is also in Santa Claus. It is a popular theme park.

Schuyler Colfax

Thomas Hendricks

Charles Fairbanks

Thomas Marshall

Dan Quayle

• Five United States vice presidents formerly represented Indiana as governors, U.S. senators, or members of the House of Representatives. They included Schuyler Colfax (served 1869-1873); Thomas A. Hendricks (1885); Charles W. Fairbanks (1905-1909); Thomas R. Marshall (1913-1921); and Dan Quayle (1989-1993). Indiana State Road 9 is nicknamed "Highway of Vice Presidents." Three vice presidents—Hendricks, Marshall, and Quayle—lived in cities along the road.

DID YOU KNOW?

PEOPLE

James Dean (1931-1955) was one of the best actors of his generation. During his short life he practically invented modern "teenage cool." Born in Marion, Indiana, he started his acting career in television commercials and dramas. His big break came in 1953's Hollywood drama *East of Eden*. He cemented his reputation in 1955's *Rebel Without a Cause*, in which he played an emotionally troubled teenager. He starred in just one other film, 1956's *Giant*. It was released after Dean's fatal 1955 automobile accident. He was just 24 years old when he died. In 1956, Dean was given a posthumous Academy Award for Best Actor.

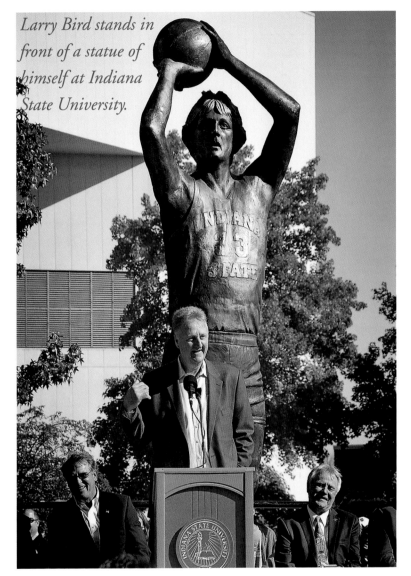

Larry Bird stands in front of a statue of himself at Indiana State University.

Larry Bird (1956-) is a retired superstar of the National Basketball Association (NBA). He was born in West Baden, Indiana, and was raised in nearby French Lick. He played high school and college basketball in the state before turning pro in 1979. He played for 13 seasons with the Boston Celtics from 1979-1992. As a forward, Bird was one of the best scorers, passers, and rebounders in the NBA. He won many Most Valuable Player Awards and was named an All Star nearly every season he played. He led the Celtics to three NBA Championships in 1981, 1984, and 1986. After retiring, he returned to his home state to coach the Indiana Pacers from 1997-2000. He was named NBA Coach of the Year in 1998. In 2003, he once again returned to the Pacers, this time as president of basketball operations.

Orville Redenbacher (1907-1995) was born in Brazil, Indiana. He grew up on his family's farm, sometimes selling popcorn from the back of his car. (Indiana is one of the country's leading growers of popcorn.) Redenbacher attended college at the state's prestigious Purdue University, where he studied

agronomy. He made it his life's goal to grow the perfect popcorn. He and business partner Charlie Bowman grew thousands of types of popcorn before finding a hybrid they at first called RedBow. It popped up large, fluffy, and tasty. They changed the name to Orville Redenbacher Popcorn to increase sales. Starting in the early 1970s, Redenbacher himself starred in television commercials for his popcorn. With his white hair, bow tie, and horn-rimmed glasses, he became a cultural icon. Redenbacher's popcorn became one of the best-selling brands in America.

Madam C.J. Walker (1867-1919) was a successful businesswoman and civil rights activist. She was the first woman to become a self-made millionaire. She made her fortune by creating beauty and hair products for African American women. Born in Louisiana, her real name was Sarah Breedlove. She suffered from scalp ailments and hair loss, which inspired her to invent hair care creams and other products. In 1910, she moved to Indianapolis, Indiana, and built a factory and hair salon for her business, Madame C.J. Walker Manufacturing Company. She sold pomades, shampoos, scalp conditioners, and many kinds of beauty products. Her company was wildly successful. She donated large sums of money to charities and scholarships, especially those that helped African Americans and the elderly. After her death in 1919, two-thirds of her fortune was left to charity.

CITIES

Indianapolis is the capital and largest city of Indiana. It is located very close to the geographical center of the state. It has a population of 848,788. Together with its suburbs and surrounding area, it is home to about two million Indiana residents. The city was founded in 1821. It is known as the "Racing Capital of the World." The city surrounds the Indianapolis Motor Speedway, site of the famous Indianapolis 500 automobile race. In the early 20th century, the city was home to many factories that made cars. Today, Indianapolis is a growing and vibrant city. It is a center of manufacturing, retail, education, and health care.

Fort Wayne is in northeast Indiana, near the Ohio border. With a population of 258,522, it is Indiana's second-largest city. It is named in honor of General Anthony Wayne, who fought Native Americans in the Northwest Territory in the 1790s. The city was founded in 1794. It began as a fort built at the confluence of the St. Marys, St. Joseph, and Maumee Rivers. By the mid-1900s, it was a booming manufacturing city. Economic hard times hit Fort Wayne in the 1970s and 1980s. Today, the city thrives, hosting a mix of manufacturing, communications, health care, financial services, transportation, and high-technology companies.

Evansville is in the southwestern corner of Indiana. It is nicknamed "River City" because it lies along the shore of the Ohio River. Founded in 1812, its population today is 120,346. It is the third-largest city in Indiana. It has a stable economy because it is home to many kinds of industries. These include manufacturing, health care, transportation, pharmaceuticals, education, and energy. Evansville has many parks, including Wesselman Woods Nature Preserve. It is a hardwood forest measuring more than 200 acres (81 ha), located totally within the city limits. Some of the trees in the park are more than 400 years old.

South Bend is in north-central Indiana, close to the Michigan border. Its population is 101,190. The city's biggest employer is nearby University of Notre Dame. The university is famous for its "Fighting Irish" powerhouse football team, and enrolls more than 8,000 undergraduate students. Besides education, other industries important to the city include health care, retail, and communications technology.

Bloomington is in the south-central part of the state. It is the gateway to the forested hills of southern Indiana. It has a population of 83,322. It is home to Indiana University Bloomington, which has more than 42,000 students. Besides education, other major employers include health care and advanced technology. Theater, live music, and other performing arts are popular in Bloomington.

TRANSPORTATION

Indiana is called the "Crossroads of America." The state has about 97,553 miles (156,996 km) of public roadways. Interstates 65, 69, 70, and 74 all converge on Indianapolis as they cross the state. Interstate 64 travels across the southern part of Indiana near the Kentucky border. Interstate 94 crosses the northern tip of the state, passing through the city of Gary.

Railroads have helped people in Indiana transport heavy goods since the late 1830s. Today, the state has about 5,347 miles (8,605 km) of track connecting Indiana's ports with cities across the state. Most of Indiana's rail traffic is freight, although Amtrak does offer passenger service.

An Amtrak train at Union Station in Indianapolis, Indiana.

Iron ore is unloaded from a ship onto waiting train cars at the Port of Indiana-Burns Harbor, on the shore of Lake Michigan. The ore will be used in the production of steel.

Indiana has more than 400 miles (644 km) of waterways that cargo ships can use. The Port of Indiana-Burns Harbor is a deepwater port. It is on the shore of Lake Michigan, near the towns of Burns Harbor and Portage. Freighters bring iron ore and coal for use in nearby steel mills. There are also two ports along the Ohio River. One is in Mount Vernon, the other is in Jeffersonville.

There are 114 airports in Indiana. The state's major airports include Indianapolis International Airport, Fort Wayne International Airport, Evansville Regional Airport, and South Bend International Airport. Indianapolis International Airport handles more than 8.5 million passengers each year.

NATURAL
RESOURCES

Indiana has more than 58,000 farms. Combined, they occupy about 15 million acres (6 million ha) of land. That is about two-thirds of all the land in the state. The top five agricultural products from Indiana are corn, soybeans, hogs, milk, and eggs.

Most of Indiana's 4.7 million acres (1.9 million ha) of forestland is in the southern part of the state. That is about one-fifth Indiana's land area. About 86 percent is privately owned. The wood cut down from these forests is used to make houses, furniture, and many other products. The forests are then replanted for future use.

Corn is harvested at a farm near Greenfield, Indiana.

Workers cut limestone from a quarry in Oolitic, Indiana.

Indiana is famous for the quality of its limestone. Quarries are located in the south and central parts of the state. The state rock is Salem limestone, also known as Indiana or Bedford limestone. This high-quality rock was formed millions of years ago on the bottom of a shallow inland sea. Indiana's first quarry started operating in 1827. Today, almost 2.7 million cubic feet (76,455 cubic meters) of Indiana limestone is carved from the state's nine quarries each year. Much of this beautiful stone is used on the outside of buildings. New York's Empire State Building is clad in 200,000 cubic feet (5,663 cubic meters) of Indiana limestone.

INDUSTRY

Many kinds of products are made in Indiana. The state is close to some of the country's largest consumer markets, including Chicago, Illinois. The many people in these places need products to live their lives, and Indiana is happy to provide them.

About 17 percent of Indiana's non-farm workers are employed by manufacturing companies. These firms make cars, motors, batteries, tires, medicine, electronics, and steel. Indiana leads the nation in steel production, thanks to the busy mills in the northwestern part of the state.

Indiana is part of a region called the Manufacturing Belt. It includes the northeastern United States plus the states surrounding the Great Lakes. Starting in the 1970s and 1980s, hard times hit these states. The economic downturn was caused by many things, including factory automation and high wages. Companies lost business to foreign competition that offered less-expensive goods. The steel industry was hit very hard. The Manufacturing Belt became known as the Rust Belt. Many people lost their jobs.

In the past 30 years, much of Indiana has bounced back. Factories remain open because the state has tried to help companies stay competitive. Indiana has also diversified its economy. It now attracts new businesses, such as high-technology companies, information services, and finance companies.

Blast furnace workers at ArcelorMittal, an Indiana steelmaking company.

39

SPORTS

Indianapolis Motor Speedway

The Indianapolis 500 automobile race is held each Memorial Day weekend in May. The racetrack is in a huge stadium called the Indianapolis Motor Speedway. It is in a suburb called Speedway, which is entirely surrounded by the city of Indianapolis. On race day, as many as 300,000 fans pack the stadium. Each race lasts 200 laps around the oval track, which equals 500 miles (805 km). The first Indy 500 was held in 1911. The original track was laid with bricks. That is why the stadium today is nicknamed "The Brickyard." The course today is paved with asphalt. Three feet (.9 m) of brick paving remains at the starting line for tradition.

Indiana has two major league sports teams. Both are located in the capital. The Indianapolis Colts play in the National Football League. The team has won two Super Bowl Championships. The Indiana Pacers play in the National Basketball Association. The Pacers have won many division titles.

The Notre Dame Fighting Irish take on the Indiana Hoosiers in a NCAA basketball game.

High school and college sports are big in Indiana. The two most competitive college teams are the Fighting Irish from the University of Notre Dame, near South Bend, and the Hoosiers from Indiana University Bloomington. Each university competes in many sports, but the most popular are football and basketball.

ENTERTAINMENT

Indiana has a long tradition of supporting the arts. Many important painters and sculptors have come from the state. There are more than 400 organizations that celebrate the arts of Indiana in all their various forms. Even in the state's many small towns, music, literature, and theater are celebrated. There are ballet troupes, opera companies, stage theaters, and film festivals throughout the state.

The Indianapolis Symphony Orchestra was founded in 1930. Today, it is one of the best orchestras in the country. There are also symphony orchestras in South Bend and Fort Wayne, and at least a dozen other Indiana cities.

The Indy Jazz Fest includes 10 days of concerts in Indianapolis by some of the best jazz musicians playing today. The Bill Monroe Memorial Bluegrass Festival is held each June in Bean Blossom, Indiana. It is the oldest, continuously running bluegrass festival in the world.

The Indy Jazz Fest is held each year in Indianapolis. It features 10 days of concerts held at various locations around the city.

The Children's Museum of Indianapolis features a Dinosphere exhibit. On the outside, three Alamosaurs seem to burst from the Dinosphere's walls. Inside are rare dinosaur fossils from 65 million years ago.

Interesting museums can be found in every major city in Indiana. The Indianapolis Museum of Art is among the 10 largest art museums in the United States. Its collections include more than 54,000 works of art covering 5,000 years of history. The Children's Museum of Indianapolis features a planetarium and more than 10,000 natural history specimens, including many dinosaur fossils.

TIMELINE

8000 BC—First humans arrive in Indiana.

1700s—France begins exploring and building forts in Indiana.

1783—The United States gains control of Indiana. More settlers come to the state.

1790s—Settlers and Native Americans fight.

1816—Indiana becomes the 19th state in the Union.

INDIANA 1816

1840s—Indiana becomes important as a trade and transportation state.

1861-65—The American Civil War is fought. Indiana stays with the Union, fighting on the side of the North.

1890s—Automobile invented. Carmakers flock to Indiana to set up factories.

1906—First Indiana steel mill constructed.

1950s—Indiana enters a time of great economic success.

1970s—Hard times hit the state.

1990s—Indiana bounces back with new ways of becoming successful.

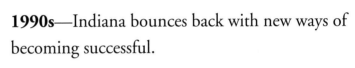

2004—The Children's Museum of Indianapolis opens *Dinosphere: Now You're in Their World*. The unique exhibit features fossils from the Cretaceous period.

2007—The Indianapolis Colts win Super Bowl XLI.

2014—Ryan Hunter-Reay wins the 98th running of the Indianapolis 500 at the Indianapolis Motor Speedway on May 25, 2014. He finished just 0.06 seconds ahead of the 2nd-place finisher, Helio Castroneves. It was the second-closest margin of victory in Indy 500 history.

GLOSSARY

Academy Award

An award presented to the year's best movie actors, writers, directors, producers, and technicians by the Academy of Motion Picture Arts and Sciences. It is also known as an Oscar, the gold statue awarded to the winners.

Agronomy

The science behind caring for soil and methods to grow crops.

Civil War

The American war fought between the Northern and Southern states from 1861-1865. The Southern states were for slavery. They wanted to start their own country. Northern states fought against slavery and a division of the country.

Deciduous Trees

Types of trees that shed their leaves in the fall.

Fertile

Soil that is able to produce many plants and crops. Indiana is famous for its fertile soil.

French and Indian War

A war fought between 1754-1763 in North America between the forces of France and Great Britain and the two countries' Native American allies. It was part of a larger worldwide conflict called the Seven Years' War.

GLACIER

A large mass of ice built up by snow that falls and does not melt at the end of winter. Glaciers can grow taller than a mountain and extend for hundreds or thousands of miles during an ice age.

INDUSTRIALIZE

To change a society or location from one in which work is done mainly by hand to one in which work is done mainly by machines.

MIDWEST

A geographic region that occupies the north-central part of the United States. It is usually defined as including 12 states: Illinois, Indiana, Iowa, Kansas, Michigan, Minnesota, Missouri, Nebraska, North Dakota, Ohio, South Dakota, and Wisconsin.

PLANETARIUM

A theater that projects the nighttime sky on a rounded ceiling, allowing people to view stars, comets, and other objects in space.

POSTHUMOUS

An award or honor given after the death of the person receiving it.

WORLD WAR I

A war that was fought in Europe from 1914 to 1918, involving countries around the world. The United States entered the war in April 1917.

WORLD WAR II

A conflict that was fought from 1939 to 1945, involving countries around the world. The United States entered the war after Japan bombed the American naval base at Pearl Harbor, in Oahu, Hawaii, on December 7, 1941.

INDEX